Sometimes Say My Name

by
Herbert Woodward Martin

Poets' Choice Publishing

Copyright © 2020 Poets' Choice Publishing
All rights reserved

Graphic Design by: Sanket Patel
Paintings by: Grace Cavalieri
Photography by: Dan Murano

Printed in the United States of America
Library of Congress Cataloging-in-Publication Data Pending
ISBN 978-1-7335400-7-0

About the Cover: "Diagnoses"
by Grace Cavalieri

Poets' Choice Publishing
337 Kitemaug Road
Uncasville, CT 06382
Poets-Choice.com

Willie Short, 36, Dishwasher

Houston, TX

"Don't forget me. Mention my name now and then."
Newsweek, August 10, 1987

"I was shot in a robbery attempt two years ago. While in the hospital, I was diagnosed as having the AIDS virus. When I came to after the operation, I saw my father whom I had not seen in 17 years. When he learned what I had, he immediately left, and I have not seen him since. Since then, I've recovered from the gunshot wound, but have suffered a much greater loss. I have lost the love of my parents and will never br a part of the family again. I have lost all my friends who have turned their backs on me. I've experienced firsthand the hatred and prejudice that come with having the disease. I've become a recluse, and have very little time left. The reason I am writing is with the loss of my family and friends, I'm afraid what will happen to me when I die.

. . . I don't want to die and be forgotten. I just want to die with dignity.

"Thanks A Million" **Percy Ross, Dayton Daily News January 29, 1988**

In Memory of William Short

Acknowledgements

Some of these poems appeared in the following journals and magazines with different margins.

I am grateful for their willingness to such visionary editors and publish these poems.

Sections I - X	*The James White Review* *Vol. 6. No.1* *Fall 1988*
Sections XI- XII; XV-XVII	*Ploughshares* *Vol. 1 No. 1* *Fall 1988*
Sections XI - XII; XV; XVII	*The Massachusetts Review* *Vol. 15. No 4* *Spring 1994*
Sections XV, XVI, XVII	*Black American Literature Review* *Vol. 23, No 3* *Fall 1989*
Section XVI	*Images* *Vol. 14. No. 1* *Fall 1981*
Sections XXI- XXVI	*The Vincent Brothers Review* *Vol. 1 No. 1* Fall 1988
Section XXXX	*The Portland Review* *Vol.36 No. 3* *Summer 1990*

About the Artist

Grace Cavalieri
Media: Acrylic on canvas
Photo Credit by: Dan Murano

Grace Cavalieri is Maryland's tenth Poet Laureate. She's the author of 26 books and chapbooks of poetry and 20 short-form and full-length plays. Her latest play "Quilting The Sun" was produced at the New Theater of New York, NYC in 2019. She founded and still produces "The Poet and the Poem" for public radio, now from The Library of Congress, celebrating its 44th year on-air.

Contents

	About the artist • vii
	Blood Path • xii
	Introduction • 2-3
	Flow • 4
I.	His mother used • 5
II.	An invisible pestilence • 6
III.	A pestilence has • 7
IV.	There is a • 8
	Stained Glass • 9
	Berries • 10
V.	Jesus was a • 11
VI.	House like humans • 12
VII.	They firebombed a • 13
VIII.	All the citizens • 14
	Transparency • 15
IX.	Fear commits disreputable • 16
X.	Mother, I have • 17
XI.	When I am • 18
XII.	This house has • 19
	Flow 2 • 20
XIII.	The cranium is • 21
XIV.	During a small • 22
	Untitled • 23
XV.	Sacrifice is the • 24
XVI.	Adam at first • 25
XVII.	This is my • 26
	Wrightsville Beach • 27
XVIII.	The frame of this • 28
XIX.	The frame of my • 29
	Escape • 30
XX.	This tender infection • 31

XXI.	The fragrance of • 32	
	Burst • 33	
XXII.	Of human flesh • 34	
XXIII.	Like all men • 35	
	BRYAN • 36	
XXIV.	The soul is • 37	
XXV.	My five advisory • 38	
	Untitled 2 • 39	
	Silver • 40	
XXVI.	The brain is • 41	
XXVII.	The house of • 42	
XXVIII.	The corpse of • 43	
XXIX.	Of all the • 44	
XXX.	House standing on • 45	
XXXI.	The house is • 46	
XXXII.	Mother, the extraordinary • 47	
XXXIII.	Sacrifice is harder • 48	
	Forensics • 49	
XXXIV.	Not hero's nor • 50	
XXXV.	When all desires • 51	
XXXVI.	The cranium is • 52	
XXXVII.	I have dreamed • 53	
XXXVIII.	Desire is a • 54	
XXXIX.	The cellar of • 55	
XL.	I request only • 56	
	Untitled 3 • 57	
XLI.	I never participated • 58	
XLII.	That Easter morning • 59	
XLIII.	So, I say • 60	
XLIV.	This is my • 61	
XLV.	This house is • 62	
XLVI.	Sacrifice is harder • 63	

	Dans Painting • 64
XLVII.	All of my • 65
XLVIII.	The cellar siphons • 66
XLIX.	When I am • 67
L.	My words are • 68 *Untitled 4 • 69*
LI.	My body is • 70
LII.	The ravaging winds • 71
	Untitled 5 • 72
LIII.	There is a • 73
	Untitled 6 • 74
LIV.	A dumb moth • 75
LV.	One significant Sunday • 76
LVI.	The body has • 77
LVII.	Turbulence is alive • 78
LVIII.	In severest mercy • 79
LIX.	See how the • 80
LX.	I never gave • 81
	Color of Berries • 82
LXI.	Easter morning when • 83
LXII.	The body is • 84
LXIII.	A punitive fire • 85
LXIV.	My home was • 86
LXV.	Let tulips surround • 87
LXVI.	A rat gnaws • 88
	Patch • 89
	Autumn • 90

A brief autobiography of Herbert Woodward Martin.

When I boarded the train from Alabama to Ohio, all the pains from those early years crowded the reflections in the windows but, that did not break the Negro conductor's concentration when he announced: "We have just crossed The Mason and Dixie Line." It was at that moment we were being promised a new kind of freedom that would prove to be subtle and sometimes confusing.

Some things changed; some things remained the same

I relished the white friends I encountered and made.

They kept me in decent employment.

They encouraged my talent for writing, and as I learned to trust them more and more, I moved from volume to volume.

My parents' motto once we became established in the North was:

"Education is the one thing no one can steal from you. Get as much as you can."

And as a result, I was the first in the family to graduate from high school and from the university, with a Masters and a Ph.D. Still, no one in the family ever felt less than worthy for who they were or what they had achieved.

Blood Path

Sometimes Say My Name

Introduction
by Richard Harteis

When I told my sculpture friend Nancy that we were about to publish a series of prose poems, she asked, "what's a prose poem?" The genre seemed to be a contradiction in terms, an oxymoron for her. In fact, this is a genre with a long history. I told her the form had rules, that such a poem needed to include the elements of poetry such as image, metaphor, internal rhythm, possibly alliteration and the sort of repetition one finds in the repeat stanzas of song. But the lyric core of such a poem is essential, despite the fact that such a cry from the heart comes in fairly routine, prosaic language.

It was all I could resurrect from my teaching days, but I needed to show her what a prose poem was, and these poems are a beautiful example of what can be achieved in the hands of a master poet whose heart beats iambic.

Herb Martin has taken the life of Willie Short as his own. These cries of one dying of AIDS are so exact, so genuine, when I mistakenly told the poet Grace Cavalieri whose art graces these poems that Herb had AIDS, she said, "Oh my God, I am crying." ("I am trying to survive the pandemic by color," she writes in a recent email.)Negative capability, Shelley tells, us is the ability to have such empathy that a poet can imagine even what it is like to be the center of a cue ball on a field of green.

I don't know how Willie Short contracted AIDS. Perhaps he was promiscuous, a hemophiliac tainted by a bad source of blood in a transfusion. It doesn't matter. He is like the thousands of ghosts who walk the earth who were simply living life in a community that had become poisoned with the corona virus. One can not be judgmental when one is facing death. It comes to us all despite the cause. But like Willie, the human hope is not to be forgotten. At the risk of being politically correct, Herb Martin has given us the life of one man whose life mattered, the universal from the particular as Aristotle would have it. This is what poetry can do, enabling us to actually see another human being, to feel his pain, to walk the lonely road of life with him a while.

In these poems one hears the lament of one whose experience is that of so many in this time in history, a new plague among us.

"Dear Lord, the young and old are dying, falling like summer insects and nobody knows whether any spraying has been done. Something secret keeps seeping into the blood, and devouring everything that is healthy. Ain't no two ways 'bout it, ain't no two ways 'bout it; something terrible is happening."

"Who is there to take on the war of the night?" the poet asks. "Who is there to keep away fear when death comes as a surprise?" Willie, like Jesus suffers at the hands of evil. "What a diligence there was when he was crowned with thorns and ransomed in the night."

Like Kubler Ross, Willie Short achieves the final insight of dying, comes to accept what is in store for him: "I request only one thing from you when I am dead. Say my name from time to time. Do not allow it to be washed away in the waters of time. Nothing floats there, not trust nor the pull of oar or a moving boat. Nothing is remembered. My life evaporates through the ague that devours my flesh. Silence will be the last dark breath I ingest. Steer me safely into the waters of a sure and resilient memory."

And like so many now who must face the dark winter we are approaching, he can only call out for help among those whose life is given to counseling us in grief. In an earlier version he writes, "Call the Rabbi, the Priest, the jack-leg Preacher, a Mullah so that they might administer some final words that I can use to introduce myself when I reach the other side. Love will serve as a conjunction and will seal my life as an act of final commitment hard as epoxy."

No, Call the poet who sings this life into memory like prophets of old, crying in the wilderness, or John the Baptist standing at the river's edge. These poems are not easy pablum to bring us peace and reassurance, though in an odd way, they do precisely that. Someone has paid the ultimate attention to a life that mattered.

When the end comes, it us understandable to think that nothing matters, that it was all for naught. But Martin gives a final vision of hope: "The Easter morning when the Roman seal was broken, it spoke of the person who had been placed in that tomb. Something otherworldly had broken the seal demonstrating spirit cannot be contained by space or time. I keep faith with an invisible kingdom where faith is an invisible reward."

SOMETIMES SAY MY NAME is a remarkable achievement, a hard-won, clear-eyed vision of life's end in the life of Willie Short. There is no book like it in poetry or prose anywhere. It is the song of Lazarus. Say it again: Willie Short, Herb Woodward Martin.

Flow

I

His mother used Castor's Oil for everything in sight, for somethings which were in sight, and for some things which were never going to be within sight. Castor's Oil could clean house even a small house of comfort whose floorboards remind you of a painful history and promised immortality. His mother was not promised anything. She lived in a house where the crevices splintered away under a fine dust. She always said: *if you clean with Castor's Oil, you will discover a fine cleanliness.* You will discover a fine cleanliness. That oil will not dry away or crack when the cold freezes its inhabitants. It is like a passion sculpting away at a rock; it is the pumice that softens the unfaithful lover. Remember to keep it away from light and heat; its odor is gravely felt.

Lord, Mama is what you saying true?

Child, she huffed and puffed, *we knew what was true before the scientists knew what the answers were, you need to listen a bit more carefully to that which is naturally said, and then you act. True is true, always will be; lies are like poison ivy and you have to chop and chop until you get the last part of the root, and as soon as you turn your back it's poking its smallest leaf out of the ground somewhere else to continue to give you trouble. Fire is the rightful enemy of every illness. God is right, Child. Fire is the only way to root out poison. You see water only worked once and then the people started acting ignorant again. Now he has got to come back here and do the job again with fire! Fire, I'm telling you.*

II

An invisible pestilence silently invaded everything. His mother promptly said, *Now, you know what that radio man ought to have said is: there are some fast gals and some mannish boys roaming these streets these days. What they need to have prescribed for them is a purgative, something that will march through them like Hitler's s First Battalion, and leave them so weak that they have to come to their senses. No.3 Castor's Oil can do the job. It's the kind of that they use to get a tank working properly, the kind of oil that gets everything lubricated and working just fine.*

Nowadays, these children have got to have a substantial plate of food placed before them even when they have no intentions of eating everything on that very plate. Lord, when I think of the opportunities placed before these kids, that I didn't have, I just have to sit here, collect my thoughts and say, "Thank You, Jesus! Some of these children are simply in too big of a hurry. I hope that the Lord, simply, don't take away the light, and leave us all in the dark, because we have been in the dark too long, and ice moves through my vessels and I turn into shudders."

III

A pestilence has come, and it looks like it has aimed all of its trouble at the young men, the smart, and even a few of those whose blood ought to have a sufficient time to have cooled. When you get to be my age…when you come to dying, you ought to have only one serious thing on your mind and that is heaven. You ought to be familiar with the bright promise of eternity. Will they finally say that this disease is a plague in the blood, and that it acts like a handsome thief who breaks in your house and still cannot find where you have stored your excess funds because no one is at home to point out where to look and so he takes revenge on the house, the walls, the floors the windows. Fury is the residue of the poison he leaves behind. The house alone cannot fight back, nor defend itself. It can only keep record.

IV

There is a certain truth about this house: about the touches it has received and about the touches it has given, the generous hugs and kisses which have transpired between givers and takers. Sometimes, the wood breathes faster than it is supposed to. Sometimes, the electricity is stretched beyond its capability. *Go to the sink and wash your body with fire, let the flames embrace your skin, let the flames introduce themselves to you, become aware of their texture, let the flames soothe your temperament, then let the water run until it is cool.*

When you have cool water, bring me a drink. How many times was I sent back to the tap and instructed to allow it to run until it was cooler. Bring it when a chill exhilarates the glass, you can feel the chill, it will run up your arm like a bolt of sudden electricity. Bring it then, it will be cold.

Dear Lord, the young and old are dying, falling like summer insects and nobody knows whether any spraying has been done. Something secret keeps seeping into the blood, and devouring everything that is healthy. Ain't no two ways 'bout it, ain't no two ways 'bout it; something terrible is happening.

Stained Glass

Berries

V

Jesus was a bright and mercurial savior; he dressed himself in human affliction and prepared himself to suffer Old Eden's rebellion. Look how they rewarded him! They slapped him with human spittle, hammered his skin to public wood, rubbed his tendons beyond the pain we experience as humans, speared his blood and watered the ground and made it sacred.

Who is there to take on the war of the night? Who is there to keep away fear when death comes as a surprise? What a diligence there was when he was crowned with thorns and ransomed the night.

VI

Houses like humans have physical aches and pains attended by generous chills. They suffer which the chinks in the walls unannounced like age that does not affect change and brings with them the torments found in the blood. They exit through the same pores that birth came through. These are the sweet ills which affect houses.

VII

They firebombed a house today Mama. Burnt it all down. And that house was owned by white people. Now those poor souls have nothing. Burnt them out of house and clothing. You could hear the age and pain of that house crackle and scream. There was nothing but smoke and flames licking at the dark chills of that house. All the town's best citizens came to watch that fire, even the local census man.

The roof burned like black tar thrown on a lynched body. It ran down the sides of that house like oil fueling a fire. The windows went ping like you said the eyes of that black kid did when they lynched him years ago. You should have seen us all moving back to a safe distance. It took the firemen a long time to respond. Someone must have thought that the fire would cure this scourge that's going around from tender to tender, and that all that they would have to do is sprinkle a little water and all would be well and the fire would be out. Disaster does not die that easily.

VIII

All the citizens whispered that that house wasn't like any other house. It was a penitentiary of worry. Now here is nothing left but ash and blame. Rich and poor white and yellow red is the grief that is left. It is the people who are left that have to move in places like that. They are the courageous salmons who brave the rushing waters, to swim back to the place where they were born where they were spawned and then repeat the cycle and die. What a casual circle! Worry is set upon us by God or Satan; one or the other is to blame. Over and over it is something rare in us that makes us dare the marrow deposits in our bones to root and grow. This is the purposes of all houses.

Transparency

IX

Fear commits disreputable acts They bring shame; if this place is thoughtful it will never touch the skin. There are some fevers that fire cannot cure; some deaths are airborne. Suspicions is a relative to each of us. It frames us among the nature of being. We must be diagnosed just as all things are diagnosed. Burning one single home will not cure this fever. The cure is in the fear we wait for.

X

Mother, I have made a gentleman's agreement with these curtained windows, and these papered walls, where the sun instills imaginary shadows, the wind gives them shape, and the dust buries them in the house as we all come and go freely. Shape is the promissory note; I move civilly through these rooms which are not of my making. This place is a carpeted bargain. I say what I need to say. I have kept faith with this shelter, the walls and the floors. I keep no secrets from them; I have shared everything with them in the light of day and the dark of night.

XI

When I am dead, hide my eyes from the curious eyes, and let my body return to its initial dust where no sun or air may disturb. My last act as a human is to pique the consciousness of the native beings. House that I nurtured, the time has arrived for you to nurture me!

I stand clear of the pariah's arena; I entered full well knowing the dangers which thrived there. It is too late to turn around. I am aware of my natural enemies. House to whom I gave my youthful energy, I now ask that you sustain me.

XII

This house has its own purposed emotions. It knows how death is acquired. The walls of this house are a quartet of feelings. The harmonies are set in conflict with each other. Each room is a single instrument that is played by a master. Each single instrument is tuned to a single pain. What is the ground rhythm which holds everything together? What is the strong pulse of song that pervades the blood and circulates from heart to brain from bone to bone. The body is the territory which must be discovered. He who is dying understands.

The skull knows the eyes of reason. Anger prevents you from standing on the edge of logic. Still you must go there before you die. It is where you will want to utter the name of your last lover before you expire.

The kitchen is where you met for genuine warmth. It was the only room you could be certain of. It was always filled with laughter. The bedroom was a clinical place; it was a place of passion. When I die, will some one who cares gently close my eyes?

Flow 2

XIII

The cranium is attic to my brain. The spine encases the electrical current. The veins respond to the dangerous joys at the ends of the synapses. That is where emotions explode. We lie among the aggravated molecules of dust, so invisible that even the eyes of a physician find it difficult to locate. There is isolation in this dying body. Whatever attacks the bodily system: cells nerves, bones, blood and finally erupts in sores that no balm can ease nor cure. What once was an irrepressible itch is now a patch of sores inhaling death.

XIV

for Poland

During a small minimal of time in the agony of my life, I saw old women kneel down believing that such an act would bring salvation to their country. They kissed the earth that surrounded the houses that they lived in. That was a gentle and tender time; they would not love that land less because some General had made a decree they could not abide nor live with. It was the old women who called the citizens to arms saying: *We have prayed long enough for the gentle necessities to house the precious water that will redeem us. The land needs it. We must return with the gentleness of our bodies and declare a new state.*

Untitled

XV

Sacrifice is the mother of superstition; ambition is the father of visions. The skeletons are the bodily frame of all houses. Be careful how you employ your voice in those rooms to cut, persuade, charm, and destroy to stay the violence that snakes off the tongue. Stand still as a rock in the dumb night, be silent as a tomb embracing the dead. Be secretive as water moving in an underground cavern. Be secretive as lava.

XVI

Adam at first fathered his seed for the earth; he secured our names for the rocks; he brought forth a precious force to make the land compatible. He planted good between desire and sacrifice. He was the first emblem of good.

XVII

This is my Spring intent; planting is my Summer initiative. The Autumn will caress my desolate prayers, the Winter freezes everything that grows with a stillness. We ask for stability for the voice to be born in the Spring weeds. May not all of our Summer efforts turn into the straw of the coming Fall. Suddenly as if the wind stopped breathing, I fall free from the flesh of the first tree.

Wrightsville Beach

XVIII

The frame of this house is made of bone, each plank is attached with cartilage and woven together with electrical nerves, arteries, veins and tissues that respond to the messages in tandem that are sent from the spine to a responsive brain. Motion that cleanses the heart does not belie the other functions of this house. It perceives the function of all houses and exerts the houses needs. The brain and heart of all houses simply comply to the demands and needs. I know this as I begin to die.

XIX

The frame of my house is built out of steel and surrounded by an electrical network where messages move like the intent of blood. Such movement moves toward and through the heart and brain to keep its functions stirring and alive. Such is the ordinary function of ordinary houses. It is the house that exerts its requirements, the heart and brain simply comply. I say this again as I lay dying.

Escape

XX

This tender infection dominates all of my organs; it carries its pain as if it were a studded crown that amazed all who saw it with its severe jewels and polished metal in which one may see many faces and other worlds. This is a quiet and human disease that awaits the dying and slowly debilitates their will. There is no restraint beyond the dark plague that alights upon the skin waiting for the arrival of death.

XXI

The fragrance of violence blooms on the presence of a gowned woman moving down an elegant staircase. The energy of this house follows her. It has mastered the demanding particulars of this house. History is a beginning, the flowering of a murderer's memory abandoned in this house a century ago. It is that same mystery that threatens my nature.

Burst

XXII

Of human flesh, of skeletons all linked together by human desires, the sections of my brain which are called into question about the wonder of life itself. The wonder of it all, the trembling of the flesh at adversity, the worry that the heart encourages, and the wrong decisions made. Why does this frail body loose all of its strength while the rhythms of its systems grow slower and slower? Still my mother grips my hand because of the possible.

XXIII

Like all men are linked, the skeleton is also bound bone by bone and appendage by appendage to flesh and desire. The brain meditates upon this prospect; the heart realizes how slowly and slowly the body's strength slips into the hands of silence.

BRYAN

XXIV

The soul is criminal; the bones its henchmen; the flesh is warden. Embedded deep within the hollows of temptation lingers the sweet taste of desire, the colorful frosting of the holiest parts of nature. Love is the most sacred of adventures mother. I know son, I know!

XXV

My five advisory faculties cement me to the ground like public sculptures. My radical desires are always appended like the ghosts of dangers which haunt my every aspiration. I know that the best way to avoid adversity is to try and pastor my hungers and to shepherd those thoughts that occur first, in my brain is to stem the tide of their aggression and keep them away from the opening that leads into a respectable heart.

Untitled 2

Silver

XXVI

The brain is cement to reason; the heart is an appendage to desire. I have tried to walk the sheer paths of the seasons and regulate the quests I will give answers to and the formulated answers why. The question always was: *How shall I feed my human greed? How shall I temper the body's nervous requirements?*

XXVII

The house of abstinence was on the road of the crooked mile and stood by a crooked stile; it had a male child in that crooked place who fell in the narrow embrace of death. He was told to use water like a simple piece of lace to line his coffin with so that when he was washed and clean we could lay him in his coffin and place him in that popular place call the ground.

XXVIII

The corpse of the man came from an extraordinary house; his skeleton was the radical frame which contained his soul. There were many entrances and numerous limited exits to his thoughts and his body were subject to the ration of limited time and sleep.

XXIX

Of all the frightful hymns the elders used to sing, sing the first one found in the church hymnal when I die. Let that music take flight with my weary prayers. Do not let the song feel anguish or rotate in the sanctuary; do not let it sour the memory. Let it pray for sweet pardon and forgiveness; let it be done with this body.

XXX

House standing on soft rock is not a safe place to occupy; you may not survive those five ancient elements should they flood the land. A rat will nibble at any brilliant foundation; it will threaten the very chill and damp of the structure, an old presence, an uncontrollable itch that can only be eased of the fingers sharp rub. I am prepared to partner voracious death. Nothing seduces like desire. Nothing seasons the flesh like salt. Nothing can preserve the flesh like salt. Say my name from time to time.

XXXI

The house is a substitute for the ordinary place we deposit the criminals of society. If we forget them it becomes a burial place for skeletons. There is but one entrance to a grave, there are numerous invisible exits. The body must learn to endure the place where it finally falls asleep.

XXXII

Mother, the extraordinary thing about this house is its soft places, its unstable darkness and the window panes that are willing to reflect the insistence of the rising morning light which falls upon voracious appetites, that hunger for the seven full course dinner with aperitif, desert and death. Desire salts and seasons the flesh.

XXXIII

Sacrifice is harder on the bones than indulgence is on the heart, ardent adversity is trouble in the blood; blindness is the dark pasture of the nerves where the five wits sentence the convicted body and rails madly against nightly pleasures. It is Cassandra who speaks to human ears or those who are attentive. Suspicion bleaches the lily; pain is the green growth of ivy. Like ivy the earth will grow a few malleable things.

Forensics

XXXIV

Not hero's nor martyr's, nor saint's desire, nor their divine intercessions can ease the daily passions that men are subject to, nor save them from their outrageous ambitions when they try to bargain with the gods. It does not matter if they are standing on impartial or holy ground.

XXXV

When all desires turn into water my physician says that the body can expire. When a mere hot flake of volcanic ash falls irretrievably toward a spider's web the dust can ignite and all alertness catch on fire. That begins the end of mortal life as we know it says my physician.

XXXVI

The cranium is my tabernacle of prayer; the scrotum is my apocalypse of anger. Beneath my fertile skin there is a shelter for malignant genes. In the circumference of my cells there is a richness. No man alone should be privy to death. I might have donated generously to love, but I was forbidden to do so. I bequeath nothing except bankrupt death.

XXXVII

I have dreamed of my sexual prowess exploding upon the world as if it were an all encompassing explosion of desire, a passionate climax, a pianissimo of breath, a glissando of farewell, a murmur of night praise and the joy of calming down. Death is the thief of all bodily desires; it is the gentlest of accomplices. They will be my inheritors and they will turn me into dust despite this treaty written on the parchment of our tongues.

XXXVIII

Desire is a wild horse; no man using a bridle may reign her in. She will not relinquish her spirit to human hands, nor will she submit to harness, rope, or to the stream where the wild waters flow. Her hooves have learned the roads of passage where the wild wind moves. Fire is the speed in her legs. The earth cannot resist the pressure of her feet

XXXIX

The cellar of this house has many siphons filled with damp remorse. Deep in the foundation where sleep is rare, my remains can be found growing with the texture of unfamiliar dreams. I know that there is something more, and I will dream of it before I die.

XL

I request only one thing from you when I am dead. *Say my name from time to time.* Do not allow it to be washed away in the waters of time. Nothing floats there, not trust nor the pull of oar or a moving boat. Nothing is remembered. My life evaporates through the ague that devours my flesh. Silence will be the last dark breath I ingest. Steer me safely into the waters of a sure and resilient memory.

Untitled 3

XLI

I never participated in a faithless kiss; my tongue was always a voluntary participant. In the midst of an unseasonable truth, I embraced a solitary silence. I have kept faith with my bodily pursuits in this afflicted house. I protest nothing.

XLII

That Easter morning broke the seal of who was buried in the tomb Joseph gave to Christ when he died. The Roman Law announced the official law requiring all dead bodies to be placed in an official place. Nothing was allowed to break that earthly command. Still we know the spirit cannot be contained by space or time. Let me speak of a visionary kingdom. It's not difficult to see.

XLIII

for Gordon Richardson

So, I say my dying is a prison no longer; I have no fear of it; I have seen a bright and capable light; it has dismantled all my personal fears.

XLIV

This is my mortal house, built with my mortal hands, neither is sacred, neither is secular. There is no balm that can soothe either, no balm to wash away the detritus of affliction. There is nothing to hinder the affliction which is in my blood and painfully creeps upon my skin.

XLV

This house is an ordinary prison, its skeleton is its bars, it has many entrances, but death is its only exit. The flesh must learn which is which and which captivates and leads the body unerringly into its final sleep.

XLVI

Sacrifice is harder than the bones, indulgence is softer than the heart, and adversity is more ardent than blood understanding its blindness among a pasture of nerves waiting with its blind wits to convict, to shout madly against nightly pleasures taken in the dark street corners while mad Cassandra's cries falls upon inattentive ears. Suspicion bleaches the lily; pain drains the green of the growing ivy. Still I am hopeful that the earth will continue to grow a few malleable fruits while death continues to reflect my voracious appetite. I continue to rely upon seven full courses with *aperitif, cordial, dessert and death.*

Dans Painting

XLVII

All of my human desires will evaporate like desert water. My physician has informed me: *You will die. I cannot save you. You are becoming a flake of volcanic ash falling towards some spider's web which will hold you with molten alertness.*

XLVIII

The cellar siphons off the poisons of this house. It will always be filled with remorse that lingers in the foundations where sleep is rare and contentment is never found. The stones will turn to dust and nothing about my existence will seem familiar unless you *say my name* repeatedly as if it were something important and not the texture of an occasional dream. There is nothing more to say.

XLIX

When I am dead, I ask one significant thing of you: *repeat the rhythms of my name. I hope that it will suggest the rhythm of life. Do not let my name fall into a tunnel of silence. Nothing is there. There is neither the thrust nor belief in life. Life is something that evaporates through the ague of my skin. Let quiet be the last dark breath I take. Steer my name into the safe waters of a sure memory.*

L

My words are filled with a drunken anesthesia; the evening does not recognize pain, it is non-existent to it. They are bark chips, dead grass which once softened my wayward footsteps. Now my wandering is confined to this bed and afterwards to a coffin where even my solitary words will not be blessed or comforted by death.

Untitled 4

LI

My body is the wreck of geography of a foreign country. Its language is incomprehensible. The landscape grows thin and emaciated. It is a place of sores and discomfort. My tongue has become the noun of naming. My heart is a verb of repentance. My eyes are immaculate adjectives and love is a conjunction with death.

LII

The ravaging winds are brief passions. They seem swifter than wholesome sins. I am a faulty fragment that you see before you. I cannot stem the water from Noah's Flood nor extinguish the promised fire that is scheduled to come.

Untitled 5

LIII

There is a winter in the wind,
fight as the body will
to combat chills or the
locks set for the bones.

Spring is a catalogue,
the heart is a ravine,
fight as the body will
against breathes and volcanoes.

Summer is a cataract
fight as the body will
nothing is permanent
change occurs day by day.

Autumn is a terrible decline
chaff is the body's will
and I am its terminal shadow
I take to the air naturally.

Untitled 6

LIV

A dumb moth with fragile wings has maneuver its way through a small crevice. I understand the sweat of friction. By invitation, I comprehend the use of fire whose tongue has licked at all my human emotions.

LV

One significant Sunday, the people gathered and there were psalms and garments strewn all over the streets where Jesus traveled. Human yells were tossed into the midday. Faith was triumphant, adulation became a cloak of deceit. He, who came on an ass, smote subterranean death and I have been fearlessly redeemed.

LVI

The body has its natural limitations, adversarial demons ravage my human blood and desires are my enemies as well. My impudent prayers cry out for a hand that can redeem a man's sins. I realize how miserable life can be.

LVII

Turbulence is alive in my bones. My cells, my synapses, corpuscles, arteries, and veins all recognize the mortality of the flesh. It announces my natural end.

LVIII

In severest mercy, burn this body; in blessed forgiveness temper this body as one might temper steel or iron ore. Heat it, melt it, burn it into malleable substances; boil and cool and separate it from its impurities. Make this body into a shape that can endure redemption.

LIX

See how the severest winds shift around that tree. Look where the bark has been slashed. See the gashes; see the holes. Those wounds did not ask for mercy, nor did they cry out of anguish. Look at the hope which bleeds from those wooden wounds.

LX

I never gave a faithless kiss. My lips and tongue were always engaged. I tell you this unseasonable truth because it is filled with diplomatic silences, bodily pains and afflictions that originated in this secular house. I protest nothing which my flesh tried to achieve.

Color of Berries

LXI

The Easter morning when the Roman seal was broken, it spoke of the person who had been placed in that tomb. Something otherworldly had broken the seal demonstrating Spirit cannot be contained by space or time. I keep faith with an invisible kingdom where faith is an invisible reward.

LXII

This body is my mortal house, its aura is secular. There are no sacred healing balms. There is nothing here to wash away human afflictions. There is nothing here to hinder the pain which creeps upon me.

LXIII

A punitive fire burns at a furious rate in the chest of this house. It burns brightly near the heart and continues grow in depth and fury. It will continue and its temperature rises accordingly. The flesh trembles as does the fire. Then a quiet descends like a sacrificial rain. All is calm in the face of death.

LXIV

My home was once a hollow closet where all of my secret cares were stored. No light ever penetrated there. Breathing was a cautious activity. Light erased the negative darkness and destroyed the photographs of pure dreams; whatever moments I desired or secured, the rewards are summed up in death. I can hardly remember the worth of the joy I pursued. I suffocate.

LXV

Let tulips surround the acre of my coffin. Let loveliness emerge from the delirious stamen, let the silent invasion of pollen be the final testament of renewal for my flesh. Let the violet colors of these flowers rage around my coffin directing all of its brilliance toward me.

LXVI

A rat gnaws at brilliance; it threatens the flesh-tree but the itch of an old presence remains. It is something uncontrollable and cannot be executed or put to death by the sharp rub of fingernails. Voracious Partner, I leave you unnamed, I ask that you remember me and that you say my name from time to time.

Patch

Autumn

www.ingramcontent.com/pod-product-compliance
Lightning Source LLC
Chambersburg PA
CBHW040002110526
44587CB00001BA/20